Aromatherapy

for You

at Home

by

Franzesca Watson

Natural by Nature Oils Limited

First edition published 1991
Revised edition published 1994
Reprinted 1995
Reprinted 1998
Reprinted 2000

ISBN 0 9521068 1 7

Published by:
Natural by Nature Oils Limited
9 Vivian Avenue
Hendon Central
London NW4 3UT
England

Printed by:
Hill & Garwood Printing Ltd.
Watford

ACKNOWLEDGEMENT

I would like to thank my loyal assistant, Marina Vundum, for her unfailing
patience and tireless efforts in proofreading and typing my manuscript.

i

CONTENTS

INTRODUCTION

Franzesca Watson opened The Aromatherapy Clinic in North London in 1974, and was among the first aromatherapists to offer essential oils to the public. Since then, her company, Natural by Nature Oils, has supplied fine quality essential oils for exclusive use in aromatherapy. In 1991 Franzesca further expanded with the opening of The International School Of Aromatherapy, of which she is Principal.

Franzesca's emphasis has always been on the safety of using essential oils. This booklet is intended as an introductory guide, to provide clear and concise information and instructions to help the beginner to use essential oils safely at home.

Essential oils are readily available, mainly at health food shops. It is important to follow instructions carefully before using these precious concentrated plant essences.

Franzesca Watson
London 1991

WHAT ARE ESSENTIAL OILS?

Essential oils from aromatic plants are fragrant and volatile. They are highly complex mixtures of organic compounds and can have up to 500 different constituents. They are derived from different parts of plants such as flowers, leaves, seeds, fruits, woods and roots.

Principally, most of the oils are extracted by steam distillation, those from citrus fruits by pressing and those from delicate flowers by solvent extraction. The consistency of the oils varies from being watery to having a rich thicker texture, and are not greasy. They readily mix in vegetable oils and dissolve in alcohol. However, they do not dissolve in water.

The colours of essential oils range from yellow to green, blue, orange, red, brown and colourless. The fragrance from each oil also varies and can be fruity, minty, musky, woody or spicy and others have exotic floral aromas. Each plant differs in the amount of oil it yields [this is reflected in the price].

The first encounter with aromatherapy can be confusing as the properties of some essential oils overlap. In this respect, there may be a choice of four or five essential oils to treat one specific disorder. Essential oils regulate the metabolism and balance the mind and body. They have the ability to bring back memories and emotions.

When they are inhaled, the aroma sensitises the olfactory nerves in the nose and has direct access to the brain, making the effect immediate. Essential oils have good skin penetration, rejuvenating the tissues and improving the elasticity of the skin, promoting the elimination of old cells and increasing the production of new cells.

They are beneficial for treating skin problems such as acne, eczema and psoriasis. The oils are cleansing and detoxifying, helping with water retention. They help to stimulate the immune system and improve the function of the circulatory system. Bronchitis, asthma, sinusitis and other respiratory conditions can be improved. Different digestive complaints can be alleviated, including constipation, indigestion and flatulence. Essential oils are also effective for treating neuralgia, arthritis, rheumatism and muscular pains.

Additionally, essential oils have antiseptic, expectorant, anti-inflammatory, antibacterial and antifungal actions. The properties of essential oils are innumerable.

BUYING ESSENTIAL OILS

When buying your essential oils it is preferable to be in contact with a supplier specializing in aromatherapy, who is concerned with the importance of purity, and is available for queries. Many brands are now flooding the country, some of which are adulterated. Only pure essential oils will give the desired therapeutic effects and synthetics cannot achieve these results.

Occasionally, essential oils can be found labelled as organic. The term "organic" implies that the plant in cultivation is grown without the use of fertilisers and insecticides. There are a few essential oils that are organic but it would be inaccurate to say that all or most are. It would be impossible to have a comprehensive inspection, as all the plants are grown in various parts of the world.

Periodically, some essential oils can vary slightly in their colour and fragrance. This is due to various factors, including climatic changes or times of harvesting. However, this variation will not affect the quality of the oils.

When purchasing your oils avoid bottles that are constantly opened by other shoppers, preferably look for essential oils bottled with tamper proof seals which protect against contamination.

Some shops may have a tester range. Generally, it is best not to evaluate more than about six oils at any one time as the odour will saturate the nose. When testing, choose an area free from odours, clear your nose before and between testing each oil. Be careful not to inhale too deeply as some of the oils can be overpowering.

Care should be taken that your skin does not come into contact with the undiluted oils. Essential oils should always be supplied in dark bottles either with an inserted dropper, or a separate glass rod dropper with a rubber teat called a pipette. The latter is more suitable in order to see the various colours of the oils and more accurate when measuring drops of oils that have different viscosities.

HANDLING AND MIXING
ESSENTIAL OILS

Mixing essential oils is not complicated but there are a few basic rules to follow. Always use clean, dried glass bottles and measuring equipment and mix your oils on a worktop that is easily washable. Essential oils can damage varnished or plastic surfaces - have paper tissues handy for spillages. Do not let essential oils come into contact with your eyes.

Empty glass bottles are available in various sizes. A 30ml bottle is a good size for body massage or a 10ml bottle for face massage. A small funnel can be useful for transferring your vegetable oils to smaller bottles. These can be obtained at your health shop or chemist. Be especially careful to replace the right dropper into, or lid on, the correct bottle, otherwise you will contaminate your oils with different odours. Remember to check that you have screwed the tops securely on each bottle after use.

If you purchase a 10ml bottle of pure essential oil, this will give you approximately 200 drops. When blending essential oils, the dilution used should be 2%. Therefore, one drop of essential oil to every 2mls of vegetable oil. For example, when using a 50ml bottle of vegetable oil, add a total of 25 drops of essential oil. This applies whether you are using just one essential oil or a combination of two or three different essential oils. If using a 10ml bottle of vegetable oil, the total amount is five drops of essential oil.

When blending an oil for the face, or young children, the amount of essential oil added to your vegetable oil should be halved, making it a 1% dilution.

When you have made your blend, gently shake the bottle to ensure the oils are thoroughly mixed before each application. Mix only the amount you require at any one time. If you wish to mix more than the required amount for future use, add approximately 5% of wheatgerm to preserve your mix from turning rancid, unless you are using jojoba as a base.

STORING ESSENTIAL OILS

Essential oils are delicate substances and are affected by strong light, heat, air and moisture. For protection they are best kept in a cool, dry, dark place. The bathroom is not suitable as it is a place of high humidity and avoid storing near heat such as radiators or cookers. Ideally, a cupboard in the bedroom would be suitable.

Do not transfer your essential oils to plastic bottles as this will interact with the chemical makeup of the essential oils, as well as causing deterioration of the plastic. When moving or travelling, containers are available to carry your oils. They are usually made from wood and are in different sizes, normally holding between 10 to 24 bottles.

VEGETABLE OILS

Vegetable oils are used for body, face and hair care. They are sometimes called carrier or base oils as they are used to dilute the essential oils. They have good skin penetration which leaves the skin nourished and feeling soft and supple. It is important that only pure, first cold pressed vegetable oils are used. Later extractions are obtained by heat or solvent processing which produce oils of inferior quality. Mineral oil (baby oil) is not recommended because it is not compatible with, and does not absorb into the skin, but lies on the surface.

ALMOND & GRAPESEED are both good basic oils for massage, grapeseed has a slightly lighter texture than sweet almond.

AVOCADO is a nourishing oil with a good rich texture. It is excellent for dry and dehydrated skin and is very good to use after sunbathing as it will moisturize the skin. During sunbathing, avocado will encourage a golden tan, but will not protect you from the ultra violet rays. Always remember to use a good sun screen when first going out into the sun.

PEACH KERNEL is not as rich as avocado but richer than almond, it can be added to almond or grapeseed to enrich your massage blend.

JOJOBA is unique as a vegetable liquid wax used as an oil. It is fine, penetrating, stable and long lasting and can be used as a face moisturizer or as a more luxurious oil for massage, being suitable for all skin types. Jojoba both conditions and restores the health of the hair. Because of its texture, it does not become sticky like some other oils and is easy to wash out. It is also ideal for dandruff and dry scalps.

WHEATGERM is very rich in texture and high in vitamin E and useful in reducing scar tissue and stretch marks. Not suited to use on its own for massage due to its thick texture and strong wheat odour. However, adding 5% of wheatgerm to your different blends will help preserve them if you plan to keep them for long periods of time.

EVENING PRIMROSE OIL improves many skin problems including nappy rash, eczema and psoriasis. It also relieves menopausal and menstrual tension, being useful for numerous disorders, including arthritis. Use evening primrose oil on its own or add to your vegetable oil or cream. Anyone wishing to obtain further information on the virtues of this oil will find many books available on the subject.

CREAMS

In addition to using vegetable oils, you can use a cream as your base. Use a fragrant and lanolin free cream made from plant products. This can be used for any specific skin problems or for creating your own personal perfumed cream. Add approximately four to six drops of your required essential oil to a 30g jar of cream. Sometimes, the oil will separate and will have to be stirred in again before using. A little jojoba, avocado or wheatgerm can be added to obtain the consistency required. Creams are ideal for creating your own perfume or moisturizer, adding the appropriate essential oils for your skin type.

For an antiseptic cream, add up to 10 drops of essential oil. This can be used for various skin problems such as cold sores, insect bites, spots, minor cuts and grazes, rashes, sunburn, etc. For eczema, a combination of four drops of camomile roman and eight drops of evening primrose oil can be used.

For certain problems it is easier to use a cream in place of a vegetable oil. In the case of thrush, applying the cream to the vaginal area, two to three times daily will soothe and give relief from the burning and itching irritation. Myrrh and cinnamon are effective against Candida albicans (which cause thrush) due to their antifungal properties, with the added benefit of myrrh having a cooling and soothing effect. Add five drops of myrrh and two drops of cinnamon to the cream. Cinnamon is a skin irritant and should always be used in a low concentration.

MASSAGE

Massage with essential oils is both physically and mentally relaxing. Not only will you benefit from the subtle and delightful fragrance, but also from the essential oils having an effect on the various systems of the body.

Essential oils penetrate the skin into the tissues and bloodstream, circulating around the body. Certain oils have a general effect whilst others have a connection with a specific organ. It can take between one to six hours before the body fully absorbs essential oils. Therefore, to obtain maximum benefit, your bath or shower should be taken beforehand.

Giving a massage is to care, it can be as enjoyable as receiving one and conveys the importance of touch.

Massage stimulates blood and lymph circulation, bringing new blood to the area being worked upon, relieving muscular aches and pains and eliminating build-up of toxins. The condition, elasticity and tone of the skin also improves.

Massage is especially good for hyperactive children, helping them to calm down and encouraging a good night's sleep.

Begin by selecting the oils you require and always remember to dilute your essential oils in a vegetable oil first. Do not assume that by using more essential oil you will obtain better results. It could possibly have the opposite effect. To create the right atmosphere, your room should be warm with the lights dimmed; play relaxing music and light your essential oil burner.

Warm your hands before starting and pour a little oil into your palms, rubbing your hands together to disperse the oils. Apply the oil to the body by starting at the lower part of the back. With your hands flat, glide up towards the neck using long smooth strokes. Mould your hands to the contours of the body and with rhythmic strokes, keep your movements flowing, avoiding deep pressure.

Keep your body relaxed and use your intuition. If you are not confident, it would be best to enrol on a short course or attend a day workshop - courses are now available in most areas.

DO NOT MASSAGE THE FOLLOWING CONDITIONS:

When there is fever or a temperature

Varicose veins

Eruptions and inflammation of the skin

Recent scar tissue

Recent fractures or dislocations

Swollen, hot and painful joints

If in doubt - DON'T

For more serious conditions, including cancer and heart problems, obtain approval from your doctor.

BATH

Bathing with essential oils is a most pleasurable way of enjoying your daily bath, having a therapeutic effect on both mind and body.

A small amount of essential oil is absorbed through the skin and inhaling the vapours at the same time has an added effect.

After running your bath water and ensuring that the water is not too hot (as the vapours from the oil will quickly evaporate) choose one or a combination of two or three different essential oils and add a total of seven drops to the water. Before immersing, agitate the water so the oils are dispersed evenly, relax and soak for 10 to 15 minutes. Using oils in the bath can be helpful in many ways. For a morning soak, use the stimulating and refreshing oils. To promote a good night's sleep, use the relaxing and sedative oils. Bathing is also useful for treating a wide range of conditions such as muscular pain and tension.

Dry skin, eczema and psoriasis can be aggravated by water and it is advisable to dilute your essential oils in just under half an eggcup of jojoba oil before adding to the bath. This same method can be used by those with sensitive skin and for children and babies. For sensitive skin and children, use only two to three drops of essential oil and for babies, only one drop. If you do not wish to dilute your essential oils in the jojoba before adding to the water, be especially careful as babies and young children love to splash and play in the bath and can easily pick up the essential oil onto their hands and if this was then rubbed into the eyes or placed in the mouth, it could cause much discomfort and lead to more serious problems.

FOOTBATH

When a bath is not available or convenient, footbaths can be very helpful. Add up to six drops of essential oil to a bowl of warm water and soak the feet for approximately 10 minutes. Essential oils penetrate through the feet very quickly and are good for conditions. such as colds, varicose veins, athletes foot, sore and painful feet and swollen ankles.

VAPORIZATION

Essential oil burners which are sometimes called vaporizers are available in different sizes, in which water and 12 to 15 drops of your chosen oil are added (remember - never let the water run dry as the burner might crack). A candle is inserted into the burner to gently warm the water and oil, which evaporates, creating the required atmosphere. Depending on the essential oils used, this can be stimulating and headclearing or calming and relaxing. The burner is very beneficial to asthma and hayfever sufferers and purifies the air to help prevent infections spreading. It is also ideal for room fresheners and for getting rid of unpleasant odours. Additionally, they make good insect repellents.

INHALATION

Inhalation is a method used whereby essential oils travel to the lungs via the nose and throat, making it useful for respiratory problems, easing sinus congestion, colds, flu, coughs, catarrh and sore throats. This method can be used once or twice daily.

Add approximately eight drops of either one or a combination of two or three oils to a bowl of near boiling water, lean over the bowl covering your head with a towel. This is also very effective for cleansing the pores of the face. Alternatively, an electric facial sauna can be used. However, only use half the amount of essential oil as less water is required.

The vapour from the oils can be very strong and eyes should be kept closed. Inhale through your nose, slowly at first then gradually breathing deeper. Breathing through the mouth will be more beneficial for throat problems. Steaming can vary either from two minutes if your skin is sensitive, or up to five to 10 minutes maximum.

Inhalation can also be used by adding a few drops of essential oil on a handkerchief. This is an effective way to relieve travel sickness or other types of nausea. The same method can be used for keeping alert when travelling on long journeys, or the handkerchief can be placed by your pillow to help deal with sleeping problems.

COMPRESS

Another effective way of using essential oils is by applying a compress. Add up to six drops of essential oil to a basin of water, agitate the water to disperse the oil evenly. Place a flannel or piece of lint on top of the water, which will collect the floating oil. Gently wring the cloth of excess water and apply on the area to be treated, wrap a towel or bandage over the compress and leave. When the compress reaches body temperature, the process can be repeated.

Use a cold compress for headaches, sprains, bruises and other hot conditions such as inflamed and swollen joints. A hot compress should be used to alleviate backaches, rheumatic, menstrual and abdominal pains and also for an abscess, earache or toothache. For urinary problems such as cystitis, apply the compress over the lower back.

NEAT APPLICATION

This method can be applied to minor burns, mouth ulcers, toothache, insect bites, warts or verrucas and nailbed infections.

When applying neat essential oil to the skin, use a cotton wool bud to treat the affected area, ensuring that you avoid making contact with the surrounding healthy skin.

ROOM FRESHENERS

There are various ways to use essential oils for room fresheners. When making fresh air sprays, add essential oils to cooled boiled water or distilled water in a ceramic or glass plant sprayer. Shake the container to disperse the oils before spraying.

Your potpourri can be refreshed and a little oil can be added to bathroom rugs. A few drops of oil on cottonwool balls is an ideal way of refreshing cupboards and drawers.

TAKING ESSENTIAL OILS INTERNALLY

In the practice of aromatherapy, it is not only the physical effect of the essential oils entering the body, but also the fragrant aspect which has a profound and significant influence.

It is unnecessary and dangerous for inexperienced people to ingest essential oils orally.

However, if anyone wishes to take them internally, it is important to realise that essential oils can be irritant to the mucous membrane and are sparingly soluble in water. It is therefore hazardous to attempt to drink essential oils mixed in water. It is also not wise to attempt to ingest them in sugar lumps.

Essential oils are mainly soluble in vegetable oils and alcohol.

ANISE STAR *(Illicium verum)* and
ANISEED *(Pimpinella anisum)*

The star anise tree is native to Southern China and the essential oil is distilled from the star-shaped fruits. The aniseed plant is a herb found in Europe and the essential oil is distilled from the dried fruits.

Both essential oils are very similar in chemical composition and therapeutic properties and are listed interchangeably in official pharmacopoeias. They have the characteristic aroma which is familiar to most people.

They are primarily digestive stimulants, particularly for aiding with digestive problems of a nervous origin. Also, they are respiratory stimulants and are helpful with breathing difficulties.

You will find them warming, antiseptic and headclearing.

This oil should be used in a low concentration.

BASIL *(Ocimum basilicum)*

The basil herb is found in most warm temperate regions of the world. The essential oil is distilled from the whole plant having a refreshing aroma, reminiscent of aniseed.

Basil is a nerve tonic having a clearing action on the mind, helpful in states of indecision and uncertainty. It stimulates the brain and improves concentration, useful for periods of long study and in cases of mental fatigue.

This oil is excellent for digestive upsets arising from nervous debility.

Basil is also helpful in treating respiratory infections.

In bathing, this oil is best used in a low concentration.

BAY (Pimenta racemosa)

Bay is a small tree growing in Mexico and the Caribbean. The essential oil is distilled from the leaves, having a warming and spicy aroma that is quite pungent and dark brown in colour.

Bay is a scalp stimulant and traditionally used to treat hair loss (alopecia) but not hereditary baldness.

It is a strong antiseptic, particularly useful in pulmonary and respiratory conditions.

BENZOIN *(Styrax benzoin)*

Benzoin is a resin which comes from tropical trees found in South East Asia and is obtained from the exudation of the trees when the bark is cut. It has a lovely sweet balsamic aroma, very similar to vanilla.

Traditionally, benzoin is used as an inhalation for respiratory congestion. Its nature is warming and drying and is suitable for all cold conditions of the lungs such as colds and flu. It is an expectorant and its actions are stimulating and energising, whilst remaining soothing on the mucous membranes.

Additionally, benzoin may be used for treating urinary problems, as it promotes the circulation of blood and the flow of urine.

Externally, benzoin is of particular value in skin lesions when there is irritation or itching, especially when the skin is cracked and dry and is also useful in treating chilblains.

BERGAMOT *(Citrus bergamia)*

The bergamot tree is cultivated in the Mediterranean region. The essential oil is expressed from the peel of the fruit, the colour being a lovely shade of green. It has a typically refreshing, citrus scent and is one of the most delicate of the citrus essential oils.

Bergamot is uplifting and being a nerve sedative, is valuable for helping with depression and anxiety states.

Useful for both overeating and improving loss of appetite, as it has a regulating action on the digestive system.

It is strongly indicated for urinary problems, especially in recurring cystitis.

Bergamot is very important in skin care, particularly for oily and infected skin conditions, also for boils, acne, eczema, psoriasis and herpes. This oil is also useful in the treatment of shingles.

BLACK PEPPER *(Piper nigrum)*

The pepper plant is a tropical vine and is cultivated in India and South East Asia for its peppercorns. As a spice, pepper is among the most important in the world. The essential oil is distilled from the berries, having an unexpectedly refined warm aroma unlike the spice.

Black pepper is mainly used for muscular aches and pains, stiffness and fatigue. Its warming and drying quality is indicated for cold conditions.

Black pepper is tonic and stimulating to the digestive tract, restoring tone to the smooth muscles of the stomach. It stimulates the spleen in the production of blood cells making it valuable in cases of anaemia. It also stimulates the kidneys, is diuretic and will disinfect the urinary system.

CARDAMON *(Elettaria cardamomum)*

The cardamon plant is native to tropical Asia. The essential oil is distilled from the seeds and has a fragrance reminiscent of ginger. Long used medicinally in India and China, cardamon is carminative and warming. It is mainly used to help digestion and is also good against colic and expels wind.
Cardamon is also effective used against nausea during pregnancy and is diuretic.

CAJEPUT *(Melaleuca leucadendron)*

The cajeput tree is native to Malaysia. The essential oil is distilled from the leaves and has a distinct penetrating camphorous aroma.

Cajeput is very antiseptic and is particularly useful for preventing infections.

It is specifically important for treating respiratory infections, whilst acting against infecting micro-organisms during a cold. Cajeput also clears nasal catarrh and soothes the accompanying soreness and headaches.

Cajeput is a very stimulating oil and its use is best avoided before bedtime.

CAMOMILE ROMAN *(Anthemis nobilis)*

Camomiles are plants common in Europe, several types being used in aromatherapy, the most favoured is the camomile roman. The essential oil is distilled from the flowers with colours ranging from blue to yellow and having a refreshing, sweet and slightly fruity fragrance.

With its strong analgesic and anti-inflammatory actions, camomile is indicated for arthritis, sciatica, muscular pains and swollen joints. When a condition is hot and inflamed, a cold compress is more suitable to use than massage.

Soothing and anti-inflammatory, camomile is excellent for all types of skin problems, when the skin is red, dry, itchy, sensitive or inflamed; valuable for eczema and psoriasis, also helping wounds, ulcers and sores.

Being gentle, soothing and calming, camomile is especially suitable for children and babies. In nursing mothers, camomile in a cream soothes sore nipples.

Camomile can be very useful for menstrual or menopausal problems and can alleviate the discomfort of cystitis.

For the mind, camomile eases states of irritability, impatience and bad temper. It is useful for anxiety, nervous tension and depression.

CAMPHOR *(Cinnamomum camphora)*

The camphor tree is native to China and Japan. The essential oil is distilled from the wood, having the typically characteristic camphorous aroma.

It is a strong respiratory and circulatory stimulant, promoting both these functions when they are sluggish and this combination makes it especially useful for the elderly. Another use is during recuperation from debilitating infections and for extreme exhaustion.

It has the advantage of being effective in treating cases of sudden shock.

Camphor is very potent and should be used more cautiously than other essential oils.

CARROT SEED *(Daucus carota)*

The carrot plant has long been used in cultivation for its edible root as a vegetable. The essential oil is distilled from the seeds having a clear and sharp aroma, unlike that associated with carrots. The essential oil of the carrot seed should not be confused with the oil obtained from the carrot root.

Carrot essential oil is a tonic for the liver and is cleansing and detoxifying.

It is very nourishing and toning for the skin.

CEDARWOOD *(Cedrus atlantica)*

The cedarwood tree is native to the lands bordering the Mediterranean and the Himalayan mountains, having an ancient use in worship and medicine. The essential oil is distilled from the wood chips and has a woody, sweet and very pleasant fragrance. Another tree called the Virginian Cedarwood (Juniperus virginiana) found in North America is now also used to produce an essential oil with the same name.

Cedarwood is a good general tonic that has a stabilizing action. It promotes peripheral circulation and stimulates the mucous membrane. It helps to compose the thoughts and centre the mind and is very grounding. Being sedative, it will relieve nervous tension.

In skin care, cedarwood is good for oily skin. It is also valuable for many scalp problems including dandruff and alopecia.

CELERY *(Apium graveolens)*

The celery plant is native to Europe. The essential oil is distilled from the seeds and has an unusual sweet spicy aroma, with the undertones of fresh celery.

Celery is a diuretic and is useful for fluid retention during a period or menopause. It is also good for cystitis. Used in the bath, celery helps with nervous fatigue especially after a tiring day at work.

CINNAMON *(Cinnamomum zeylanicum)*

The cinnamon tree is native to the Island of Sri Lanka, this species providing the best quality of cinnamon spice. The essential oil is distilled from the bark or leaves. The aroma of the cinnamon leaf essential oil is spicy and resembles that of cloves.

Cinnamon is warming and is a stimulating tonic, excellent for all forms of mental and physical fatigue and exhaustion. It is a strong antimicrobial agent, especially antifungal and of value in treating Candida albicans (which cause thrush). It is very good for treating infectious problems and aiding during the recovery period.

Specific for the digestion, cinnamon is a strong digestive stimulant and antiseptic. It is also a circulatory stimulant and astringent.

This oil is a skin irritant and should be used in low concentration.

CLARY SAGE *(Salvia sclarea)*

Clary sage is a herb found in the Mediterranean region and the essential oil is distilled from the whole plant having a heady fragrance with woody undertones.

This oil is an excellent nerve tonic, is sedative and effective when treating stress and tension and will help reduce high blood pressure.

It will improve irregular periods and help with hot flushes and emotional fluctuations occurring in the menstrual cycle.

Clary sage is antidepressant; it induces an euphoric quality to the emotions and can be powerfully heady. It should be used with care.

CLOVE *(Eugenia caryophyllata)*

The clove tree is native to the Mollucas Islands. The essential oil is distilled from the leaves, unopened buds or twigs. The oil has a warm, spicy, metallic aroma that is unmistakably associated with the dental clinic.

Clove is warming, a very strong antiseptic and is useful against infections, especially digestive but also respiratory. It is a good general stimulant relieving both mental and physical fatigue.

Traditionally, clove has a reputation as a topical remedy for toothache, a drop of the essential oil being applied directly to the cavity in the tooth. It is also good as a rinse for sore throats and to freshen the breath.

Clove is both analgesic and antiseptic making it useful for infected wounds or sores, arresting the infection and soothing the pain.

It is customary to use clove as a moth deterrent and can also be used to repel wasps.

CORIANDER *(Coriandrum sativum)*

Coriander is a herb native to the Mediterranean region. The essential oil is distilled from the dried fruits, having a crisp and spicy fragrance.

Coriander is a digestive stimulant and carminative promoting digestion and preventing flatulence. It improves the appetite and is useful in the treatment of anorexia.

This oil is warming, analgesic and antispasmodic making it good for rheumatic and joint pains.

CYPRESS *(Cupressus sempervirens)*

The cypress tree is found throughout the Mediterranean region. The essential oil is distilled from the leaves, twigs and cones, having a woody, clear and dry fragrance.

Cypress is a powerful astringent, having a particularly strong vasoconstricting action and is very effective in the treatment of varicose veins and haemorrhoids. This same strong action is effective in checking excessive perspiration, including that of the feet. It is also a good circulatory tonic.

During menstruation, cypress will help ease heavy periods by its regulating action.

Cypress is particularly helpful in treating bronchial and asthmatic problems. Steam inhalation should always by avoided during an asthma attack. However, a few drops of cypress on a handkerchief is recommended.

In skin care, the astringent action of cypress makes it suitable for oily skin.

EUCALYPTUS *(Eucalyptus globulus)*

The eucalyptus tree is native to Australia. Although the whole tree contains essential oil, this is mainly distilled from the leaves, having a strong camphorous aroma that is deep and penetrating.

Eucalyptus, mostly used as an inhalation, is a strong antiseptic particularly useful for all kinds of nose, throat and respiratory tract infections, including sinusitis, tonsillitis and catarrh and offers good protection from flu.

Having antiviral properties, the oil is effective in treating cold sores, shingles and chickenpox. It is also a useful oil when there are outbreaks of head lice.

FENNEL *(Foeniculum vulgare)*

Fennel is a herb native to Europe and the essential oil is distilled from the seeds, having a sweet aniseed aroma.

It is a tonic to the digestive system, strengthening the intestines and is effective in treating all forms of digestive disorders including indigestion, flatulence, colic and constipation.

Fennel is a very good diuretic, used for dealing with urine retention and this makes it helpful in some cases of obesity. The detoxifying actions of this oil are valuable in helping the body cleanse itself and in particular by promoting the excretion of alcohol from the body.

Both the diuretic and detoxifying properties make this an excellent oil for treating cellulite.

Fennel is also very useful in menopausal problems due to its regulating effect on the female reproductive system. It stimulates the production of oestrogen, helping to stabilize hormonal level fluctuations and increase the milk flow in nursing mothers.

FRANKINCENSE *(Boswellia thurifera)*

The frankincense tree is native to Yemen and East Africa, exuding a resin from its bark. The essential oil, which is sometimes called olibanum, is distilled from this resin, having a fresh, clear, penetrating and comforting fragrance.

It is traditionally used for religious services. Frankincense has the ability of deepening the breath, inducing a state of concentration and is especially useful for meditative purposes. Additionally, it can be used for many respiratory problems, including asthma.

Frankincense also has a protective quality to help the individual deal with exposure to extremely stressful situations.

This is an excellent oil for treating wounds, promoting the healing process.

In skin care, it is especially indicated for mature skin, toning and fortifying the skin and improving its texture.

GERANIUM *(Pelargonium graveolens)*

Geraniums are herbaceous plants native to South Africa. The essential oil is distilled from the leaves but has such a deliciously sweet, floral fragrance, it smells more like an essential oil obtained from flowers.

An important quality of this oil is that it is balancing and regulating. Geranium has a very pronounced effect on the emotions, being antidepressant and uplifting and due to the balancing actions, is sedative in anxiety states.

Geranium is good for both premenstrual tension and menopausal problems due to the ability of stabilizing hormonal fluctuations. It is gently diuretic, relieving excessive fluid retention.

In skin care, geranium has a mild tonic action, suitable for almost all skin types. The regulating effect on the production of sebum makes it particularly good for excessively dry or oily skin. It is very cleansing, refreshing and especially soothing on inflamed skin.

GINGER *(Zingiber officinale)*

A herbaceous plant native to South East Asia. The essential oil is distilled from the rhizome and has a deliciously warm, spicy aroma.

Ginger is warming and drying and particularly suitable for treating conditions caused by exposure to cold and damp. This makes it valuable for treating rheumatism, muscular aches and pains, colds and flu.

Ginger is effective in relieving stomach cramps and other digestive upsets. Additionally, different types of nausea, including morning and travel sickness can be alleviated.

HYSSOP *(Hyssopus officinalis)*

The hyssop herb is native to Southern Europe. The essential oil is distilled from the whole plant having a cold, medicinal aroma with sweet undertones.

Hyssop has a strong decongesting action on the lungs, alleviating mucous build-up, fighting chest infections and improving breathing. This oil is good for hayfever and sinusitis.

A general and circulatory tonic, hyssop is an excellent blood regulator and strengthens the system when in a depleted state as during convalescence.

Hyssop has a clearing effect on the mind by helping to release clinging thoughts.

HO LEAF *(Cinnamomum camphora)*

Ho leaf essential oil comes from the same tree as camphor. The essential oil is distilled from the leaves, and resembles rosewood essential oil. Their therapeutic properties are also very similar, helping to clear the mind and aid concentration.

JASMINE *(Jasminum grandiflorum)*

The jasmine plant is native to the East and was introduced into Europe during the 16th century. The essential oil is obtained from the delicate flowers by solvent extraction and is a deep, burnt red in colour. It has an exquisite floral bouquet with a sweetly engaging and enticing note and a sensual hint of musk.

Jasmine is calming and relaxing whilst uplifting and is a valuable oil for all states of emotional upset. It promotes an optimistic attitude and confidence, is useful in dealing with apathy and disappointment and fortifying in cases of nervous debility and lethargy.

It is a uterine tonic, valuable in childbirth and good for easing menstrual cramps and pain, also relieving post-natal depression.

In skin care, jasmine is beneficial for inflamed and sensitive skins.

JUNIPER *(Juniperus communis)*

The juniper tree is grown throughout Europe and the Mediterranean region. The essential oil is distilled from the berries having a fresh, resinous and sweet fragrance.

Juniper is a powerful diuretic, having a strong tonic and antiseptic action on the kidneys and the whole urinary system. It is useful for urinary tract infections especially cystitis and in treating scanty periods, this oil will be of help.

It is astringent and also a blood purifier, useful for septic skin conditions including acne, dermatitis, eczema and psoriasis.

The detoxifying and diuretic actions help cleanse the body of toxins and therefore, this is one of the most valuable oils for treating cellulitis.

Juniper is a digestive tonic, stimulating the appetite and improving a slow and lethargic digestion. It is valuable in convalescence.

LAVENDER *(Lavendula officinalis)*

The lavender herb is found throughout Europe. The essential oil is distilled from the flowers having the very familiar lavender fragrance.

Lavender is the most versatile essential oil with a wide range of therapeutic properties.

Its main action is that of neutralizing, balancing and harmonizing. It soothes the mind of all emotional imbalance and nervous exhaustion and is useful for general debility. It is sedating, antidepressant and will help with insomnia and headaches.

It has a tonic and sedative action on the heart, beneficial for high blood pressure and palpitations.

Lavender stimulates the immune system and protects the body from infection, also aiding the body against recurring infections.

The analgesic and cooling actions are valuable in all types of muscular, arthritic and joint pains.

In skin care, lavender promotes cellular regeneration and helps with the healing of wounds and prevention of scarring. It is valuable in treating blisters, sunburn, acne, boils, insect bites and minor burns (for this latter condition lavender can be used neat).

With its soothing and gentle actions, lavender can safely be used on babies and young children.

Lavender will enhance the action of other essential oils.

LEMON *(citrus limonum)*

The lemon tree originates in the East and is now in widespread cultivation for its fruit. The essential oil is expressed from the peel and has a clean, tangy and extremely fresh fragrance and is a very invigorating oil.

Lemon is digestive and regulates stomach acidity, easing gastritis and indigestion.

With a strong antiseptic and antibacterial action, it is effective in treating infectious conditions, especially colds, flu and sore throats. Additionally, lemon stimulates the immune system and enhances the body's resistance to infection.

Lemon has a tonic action on the circulatory system and also regulates body fluids, reducing tissue congestion and water retention, useful in treating cellulite.

In skin care, lemon is useful for oily and spotty skin types and has been used to lighten freckles. It is also helpful in treating warts, verrucas and corns.

LEMONGRASS *(Cymbopogon citratus)*

Lemongrass is native to tropical Asia. The essential oil is distilled from the whole plant, the fragrance being reminiscent of lemon but with a stronger and sweeter aroma.

It has a powerful tonic and stimulating action on the whole body and is particularly useful for treating feverish conditions.

Lemongrass is refreshing and deodorant and is a tonic for tired feet.

In skin care, lemongrass is very antiseptic and is excellent for treating acne conditions.

It is one of the more irritant essential oils and to avoid a strong reaction, it is best used in a low concentration.

LIME *(Citrus aurantifolia)*

The lime tree originates in the East but is now in widespread cultivation for its fruit. The essential oil is obtained by expression of the peel. It has a very fresh, sweet, zesty fragrance.

Lime is digestive and regulates stomach acidity, relieving gastritis and indigestion.

With very strong antiseptic and antibacterial actions, lime is useful in treating infectious conditions, including colds and flu.

MANDARIN *(Citrus nobilis)*

The mandarin tree is native to the East and the essential oil is expressed from the peel, having the typical citrus fragrance being finer and sweeter than the orange and slightly exotic.

This is the most gentle and calming of the citrus oils and is one of the few oils that is beneficial and safe to use during pregnancy.

It has a soothing effect on the nervous and digestive systems and is very good for children and the elderly; also the weak or debilitated.

Mandarin is sedative and antispasmodic and in skin care, is good for oily skin.

41

MARJORAM *(Origanum marjorana)*

The marjoram herb is native to Europe and Central Asia. The essential oil is distilled from the whole plant and has a medicinal and sweet camphorous aroma.

Marjoram is comforting to the mind, helpful in nervousness, anxiety and irritability.

It is warming and useful for all muscular aches and pains from over exertion. Its antispasmodic action also helps with muscle spasms.

Marjoram has a tonic effect on the digestive tract, aids digestion and relieves constipation.

Additionally, it is indicated for easing sexual excitement and helps to regulate the blood pressure. It warms the womb and is good for period pains.

MELISSA *(Melissa officinalis)*

The melissa herb is found in Southern Europe. The essential oil is distilled from the whole plant having a fresh, sweet and lemony fragrance.

Melissa is a gentle but potent tonic especially for the heart, being useful for strengthening it when overly strained and weakened and will gently ease palpitations.

As a nerve tonic, it is uplifting on the spirits whilst also soothing and relaxing. It is particularly suited to phases of restlessness in sensitive individuals prone to panic attacks.

This oil should be used in a low concentration.

MYRRH *(Commiphora myrrha)*

The myrrh tree is native to Yemen and East Africa and like the frankincense tree, it also exudes a resin from its bark. The essential oil is distilled from the resin, having a musky, balsamic aroma.

Myrrh is soothing for the mucous membranes and is anti-inflammatory and very useful for promoting healing in wounds. It is also effective for oral hygiene, including mouth ulcers and gum infections, when used as a rinse.

The soothing action of myrrh is supported by its antifungal property and is very good for various skin conditions, including rough and cracked skin. Myrrh is rejuvenating and indicated for preserving a youthful complexion in mature skin.

NEROLI *(Citrus aurantium)*

Neroli essential oil is distilled from the flowers of the bitter orange tree which is native to the East. It has a delicate floral and tenacious fragrance with a basic citrus note.

Neroli has a slightly hypnotic effect on the mind and is especially good for insomnia. It is very sedating to the nervous system and is useful for states of depression and anxiety and very effective for relieving stress or shock.

It has a gentle and calming action on the heart, regulating and stabilizing the contractions and is useful for sensitive people who are alarmed, apprehensive or easily upset.

In skin care, neroli is valuable for its regenerative powers in promoting cell growth and replacement. It is especially good for broken capillaries and suitable for all skin types, particularly blotchy, dry and sensitive skin.

NIAOULI *(Melaleuca viridiflora)*

The niaouli tree grows in New Caledonia in the South Pacific Ocean, just off Papua New Guinea. The essential oil is distilled from the leaves and has a penetrating but delicate camphorous aroma.

Niaouli is very antiseptic and has a strong anti-inflammatory action and similar properties to cajeput. However, as niaouli is more gentle, it would be better tolerated by more sensitive individuals.

It is specifically indicated for all kinds of throat and respiratory infections.

Niaouli promotes healing of wounds and is very effective for all kinds of skin infections, being more suitable for chronic cases requiring repeated applications.

NUTMEG *(Myristica fragrans)*

The nutmeg tree is native to the Indonesian Islands. Two essential oils can be obtained from this plant. The main essential oil is distilled from the seed and is called nutmeg, another essential oil is distilled from the covering of the seed and is called mace. The properties of both are very similar. The fragrance is spicy, sweet and warming.

Nutmeg is a particularly potent stimulant and is better used in smaller quantities than other essential oils. Its main stimulant action is on the digestive system and will improve appetite and aid indigestion.

It also stimulates circulation and is useful for rheumatic pains. Nutmeg has a very strong action on the nervous system. The spice taken in a high dose is known to induce hallucination, but used in a low dilution, is helpful for intellectual fatigue.

Occasionally, it has been effective in treating impotence.

ORANGE *(Citrus sinensis)*

The orange tree is native to the East but is now naturalised in the Mediterranean region. The essential oil is expressed from the peel of the sweet orange, having the typical citrus, zesty fragrance. It is very refreshing, exuberant and warming and is golden yellow in colour.

Orange is a digestive stimulant, improving the appetite and toning the digestive tract, useful for constipation and relieving digestive upsets caused by anxiety states.

This oil should be used in a low concentration in the bath, as it may cause skin irritation.

PATCHOULI *(Pogostemon cablin)*

Patchouli is a tropical herb, native to Indonesia and is related to the mint family of herbs. The essential oil is distilled from the whole plant, being reddish golden brown in colour. It has a very strong, warm, earthy and distinctively musky aroma and is one of the few oils which improves with age.

Patchouli is a tonic on the nerves, overcoming anxiety and depression and is very grounding.

The use of patchouli is important in skin care as it promotes new skin growth. It is very good for mature skin, helping to maintain a good texture and is suitable for skin allergies. Patchouli also aids in the healing of cracked skin and weeping sores, having anti-inflammatory properties.

PEPPERMINT *(Mentha piperita)*

The peppermint herb is found throughout the northern temperate regions. The essential oil is distilled from the whole plant having a sharp, fresh and minty aroma.

Peppermint has a strong action on the digestive tract and is valuable for all digestive problems including indigestion, flatulence, colic and different types of nausea.

It is a very stimulating, invigorating and headclearing oil and will ease headaches and sinusitis. Being a nerve tonic, peppermint is useful for anxiety and depressive states.

Its cooling effect is soothing for reddened and inflamed skin including sunburn. It is effective in relieving itching or skin irritation.

Peppermint used in a footbath will refresh and deodorize tired aching feet.

As a mosquito repellent, it is very effective.

This oil is best used in a low concentration.

PETITGRAIN *(Citrus aurantium)*

The bitter orange tree is native to the East and the essential oil distilled from the leaves and twigs is called petitgrain. Its fragrance is reminiscent of orange but differs in having a greenish hint and a woody note.

Petitgrain is astringent and tones and balances the skin. It fortifies the nerves and has a neutral action on the mind and is helpful for anxiety and palpitations.

PINE *(Pinus sylvestris)*

The pine tree is found in most temperate regions of the world. However, a superior essential oil is obtained from the pine trees grown in Siberia. The essential oil is distilled from the needle-like leaves, having a powerfully fresh and sharp aroma with woody undertones.

Pine is very antiseptic and is excellent for use as an air freshener and is an effective deodorant. The smell of pine has an invigorating and reviving effect on the mind.

It is expectorant and is specific for respiratory tract infections, making it very useful for all types of colds and flu.

In skin care and particularly in facial steaming, pine is extremely effective in cleansing the pores of the skin.

ROSE *(Rosa damascena)*

The rose plant is native to the East and the essential oil is obtained by solvent extraction from the flower petals. It has a most beautiful fragrance that is profound and elegant.

Among the least toxic oils, rose is suitable for delicate and fragile types of people as well as children.

Relaxing and soothing on the nerves, rose calms anger and aggression and eases the mind of intense emotion.

Rose is a general tonic and fortifier with a strong influence on the circulatory, nervous and female reproductive systems.

It is exceptionally useful for gynaecological problems, easing the condition through its regulatory and especially cleansing actions. It is helpful for post-natal depression.

In skin care, rose is suitable for delicate skin and mature skin, effective in preserving a youthful complexion by nourishing and restoring the skin tissues. It is mildly astringent.

ROSEMARY *(Rosmarinus officinalis)*

The rosemary plant is native to the Mediterranean region. The essential oil is distilled from the whole plant and has a sharp, warming and camphorous aroma.

Rosemary is a heart tonic and circulatory stimulant, promoting the entire blood circulation but particularly the blood supply to the brain. It helps with all mental processes, improving the memory, mental fatigue, fainting and vertigo.

It has a strong action on the circulation and helps to lower high cholesterol levels and regulate blood pressure.

Rosemary is warm and stimulating to the nervous system and is fortifying for general debility and lethargy. It is helpful in muscular tiredness, stiffness and aches and pains.

ROSEWOOD *(Aniba rosaedora)*

The rosewood tree is found in South America and grows in the Amazon rain forest. The essential oil is distilled from the wood, having an interesting aroma that is both woody and floral.

Rosewood makes a good deodorant with its light, refreshing fragrance.

It has a mild balancing action on the nerves, steadying the mind and clearing the head. This makes it especially useful when concentration is required over prolonged periods or when there is a strong tendency for the mind to drift and daydream. Its uplifting effects are also beneficial when used at times of crises to ease the unavoidable emotional demands.

SAGE *(Salvia officinalis)*

The sage herb is found throughout the temperate and tropical regions of the world. The essential oil is distilled from the whole plant having a clear and piercing camphorous aroma.

Sage is a superb general tonic suitable for all kinds of fatigue and general debility, is helpful for convalescence and is suited to people of weak constitutions.

It exerts a strong action on the blood and regulates menstruation. Sage is especially valuable during menopause as it also inhibits sweating and provides some oestrogenic type effects in stabilizing the hormonal fluctuations during this time.

This oil is best used in a low concentration.

SANDALWOOD *(Santalum album)*

The sandalwood tree is native to India and is a semi-parasite that grows on other trees and takes some of its nourishment from its host. The essential oil is distilled from the inner heart-wood and has a sweet and distinctly exotic and oriental fragrance.

The specific and very pronounced action of sandalwood is on the genito-urinary systems, making it a very powerful antiseptic in the treatment of genital and urinary infections, including cystitis. Sandalwood is a sexual restorative, soothing the mind of anxiety and tonifying the reproductive system.

This oil is also an expectorant making it of value for throat problems, including dry coughs.

Sandalwood is important in skin care, being beneficial to many different skin types but primarily for dry and dehydrated skins. It is soothing, relieves itching and is slightly astringent and anti-inflammatory.

TEA TREE *(Melaleuca alternifolia)*

Tea tree is native to the coastal regions of South East Australia. It has been used by the indigenous Australian aborigines for centuries but has only recently been introduced into Europe. The essential oil is distilled from the leaves and has a pronounced medicinal odour.

Tea tree has a very useful combination of being an exceptionally powerful antibacterial, antifungal and antiviral agent, whilst having low toxic properties. Like eucalyptus, it also stimulates the immune system and promotes protection against debilitating illness, such as glandular fever.

It is effective for treating all kinds of infectious problems, especially those of the mouth, throat, chest, skin and feet.

Additionally, its antifungal action is also effective against Candida albicans that cause thrush.

THYME *(Thymus vulgaris)*

The thyme herb is found throughout temperate Europe and Asia. The essential oil is distilled from the flowering tops having a strong medicinal aroma.

There are two varieties of thyme essential oil, red thyme and white thyme. The red thyme, after being redistilled becomes the white thyme. The red is stronger in action whilst the white is more gentle and suitable for sensitive people.

Thyme is a strong antiseptic especially of the respiratory tract. It is very effective for all types of pulmonary infections including bronchitis and bronchial catarrh. The additional antispasmodic action makes it useful in cases of asthma. It promotes resistance to infection and is also good for mouth and throat infections, coughs, colds and flu.

As a digestive stimulant, thyme will disinfect the intestinal tract. It is also useful for muscular fatigue and rheumatic pains.

VETIVERT *(Vetiveria zizanioides)*

Vetivert is a tropical grass native to India. The essential oil is distilled from the dried roots, with a rich dark brown colour and has a strong earthy, smoky aroma which becomes more subtle when diluted.

Vetivert is outstanding for its deeply relaxing effect and is most helpful with stress related states.

YLANG-YLANG *(Cananga odorata)*

Ylang-ylang is a flowering tree from South East Asia, which is very popular with the local natives for its delicious oriental fragrance. The essential oil is distilled from the beautiful yellow flowers, having an exceptionally voluptuous and extremely sweet scent. The most important property of ylang-ylang is in regulating the heart rate and respiration, improving both over and under activity. It is suitable for treating trauma caused by fright or shock, anxiety and anger, especially that arising from frustration.

It has a sedating and calming effect on the nervous system and is also effective in helping with sexual deficiencies like frigidity and impotence.

In skin care, ylang-ylang is soothing and suitable for dry and oily skin types, regulating the secretion of sebum.

EXAMPLES OF SOME USEFUL RECIPES

MASSAGE BLENDS

Constipation: (massage over abdomen and lower back)

10 drops Rosemary
9 drops Marjoram
6 drops Black pepper

Colds & Flu (chest rub)

12 drops Benzoin
7 drops Cajeput
6 drops Ginger

Muscular Aches:

10 drops Rosemary
9 drops Coriander   or
6 drops Ginger

10 drops Rosemary
9 drops Lavender
6 drops Marjoram

Painful Joints:

15 drops Camomile
5 drops Juniper
5 drops Lavender

Immune System:

10 drops Tea Tree
8 drops Eucalyptus
7 drops Lavender

Relaxing Massage:

11 drops Sandalwood
8 drops Ylang Ylang   or
6 drops Orange

11 drops Rosewood
8 drops Frankincense
6 drops Geranium

Stimulating Massage:

12 drops Juniper
8 drops Black pepper   or
5 drops Lemongrass

10 drops Pine
10 drops Lemon
5 drops Fennel

For each massage blend add 25 drops essential oil to 50ml vegetable oil.

HAIR TREATMENTS

Dandruff:

15 drops Rosemary
10 drops Cedarwood

Hair Conditioner:

10 drops Rosemary
7 drops Lemon
8 drops Rosewood

Hair Stimulant:

11 drops Rosemary
8 drops Bay
6 drops Cedarwood

Psoriasis (scalp):
10 to 15 drops Camomile

For each of the above treatments, add 25 drops essential oil to 50ml Jojoba. Rub oils between the hands, apply evenly to hair and scalp. For best results, leave overnight and shampoo next morning.

CREAMS

Antiseptic Cream:

6 drops Lemon
4 drops Thyme

Cold Sores:

5 drops Lavender
5 drops Eucalyptus

Perfume Cream:

3 drops Rose
3 drops Neroli

or

Haemorrhoids:

6 drops Cypress
4 drops Myrrh

Hand Cream:

5 drops Benzoin
5 drops Myrrh

3 drops Jasmine
3 drops Neroli

Add the above or your own choice of essential oils to a 30g jar of fragrant free cream.

BATHING

Detoxifying Bath:

3 drops Juniper
2 drops Rosemary
2 drops Fennel

Itchy skin, Eczema or Psoriasis:

15 drops Camomile to 50ml jojoba - add just under half an eggcup of blend to bath water.

Refreshing Morning Baths:

4 drops Rosemary 3 drops Bergamot	or	4 drops Juniper 3 drops Eucalyptus
4 drops Petitgrain 3 drops Lemon	or	5 drops Geranium 2 drops Orange

Relaxing Evening Baths:

4 drops Frankincense 3 drops Lavender	or	4 drops Sandalwood 3 drops Ylang Ylang
5 drops Neroli 2 drops Marjoram	or	4 drops Camomile 3 drops Clary sage

Add up to a total of seven drops essential oil to bath water.

After Bath Moisturizer:
Add your choice of essential oils to a fragrance free body lotion or a jojoba base.

Babies' Bath or Massage:
Add one drop Camomile or one drop Lavender in one to two tablespoons of jojoba oil.

Facial Steaming (see Inhalation):
Spots, blackheads and cleansing - Pine, Eucalyptus and Lavender.

VAPORIZATION (Essential Oil Burner)

Sick Room: Thyme and Pine or Eucalyptus and Lemon

Insect Repellent: Citronella, Peppermint or Clove

Room Fresheners:

Eucalyptus and Lemon	Bergamot and Rosewood
Ginger and Orange	Frankincense and Rose
Lavender and Peppermint	Geranium and Juniper
Basil and Grapefruit	Mandarin and Sandalwood
Lavender and Petitgrain	Cedarwood and Ylang Ylang
Lemon and Patchouli	Orange and Cinnamon Leaf

Lemon and Orange blend particularly well with almost every essential oil.

THE GENERAL EFFECTS OF ESSENTIAL OILS

STIMULATING	REFRESHING AND UPLIFTING
Anise Star	Basil
Basil	Bergamot
Black Pepper	Cypress
Cajeput	Eucalyptus
Camphor	Fennel
Cinnamon	Geranium
Clove	Juniper
Eucalyptus	Lavender
Hyssop	Lemon
Lemongrass	Lemongrass
Niaouli	Lime
Peppermint	Mandarin
Pine	Melissa
Rosemary	Orange
Sage	Peppermint
Tea Tree	Petitgrain
Thyme	Pine
	Rosemary

RELAXING	WARMING
Benzoin	Anise Star
Camomile	Benzoin
Cedarwood	Black Pepper
Clary Sage	Cardamon
Petitgrain	Cajeput
Frankincense	Cinnamon
Ho Leaf	Clary Sage
Geranium	Clove Leaf
Jasmine	Coriander
Lavender	Ginger
Marjoram	Marjoram
Myrrh	Nutmeg
Neroli	Sandalwood
Patchouli	
Rose	
Rosewood	
Sandalwood	
Vetivert	
Ylang Ylang	

INDEX OF DISORDERS

Disorders	Essential Oils	Methods of Application
Abscess	Bergamot.Camomile.Tea Tree.	C/CR
Acne	Juniper.Lavender.Lemongrass.	B/C/CR
Anxiety	Neroli.Sandalwood.Ylang-ylang.	B/M
Appetite (lack of)	Coriander.Fennel.Ginger.	M
Asthma	Benzoin.Cypress.Frankincense.	B/M
Athletes Foot	Tea Tree.	F/N
Blackheads	Lavender.Pine.	I
Blemishes	Frankincense.Neroli.	CR/M
Blisters	Lavender.Myrrh.	C
Blood Pressure (regulating)	Marjoram. Rosemary.Ylang-ylang.	B/M
Boils	Bergamot.Camomile.Lavender.	C/I
Bronchitis	Benzoin.Eucalyptus.Thyme.	B/I/M
Bruises	Cypress.Hyssop.Lavender.	C/M
Burns (minor)	Camomile.Lavender.	C/N
Capillaries (broken)	Cypress.Frankincense.Neroli.	CR/M
Catarrh	Cajeput.Eucalyptus.Thyme.	I/M
Cellulite	Fennel.Juniper.Rosemary.	B/M
Chapped Skin	Benzoin.Myrrh.	CR/M
Chickenpox	Camomile.Eucalyptus.Lavender.	B/CR/M
Chilblains	B.Pepper.Cypress.Rosemary.	CR/F/M
Cold sores	Eucalyptus.Lavender.Niaouli.	CR/M
Colic	Fennel.Peppermint.	M
Concentration	Basil.Rosemary.Rosewood.	B/V

Disorders	Essential Oils	Methods of Application
Confidence	Jasmine.	B/M/V
Constipation	B.Pepper.Marjoram.Rosemary.	C/M
Convalescence	Juniper.Lavender.Rosemary.Sage.	B/M/V
Corns	Lemon.Tea Tree.	CR/F/M
Coughs	Benzoin.Niaouli.Pine.Thyme.	I/M
Cramp	B.Pepper.Rosemary.	C/M
Cystitis	Camomile.Juniper.Sandalwood.	B/C/CR/M
Dandruff	Cedarwood.Rosemary.	M
Daydreaming	Rosewood	B/V
Deodorizer	Cypress.Peppermint.Pine.	B/F/M
Depression	Bergamot.Jasmine.Neroli.Rose.	B/M/V
Dermatitis	Camomile.Juniper.	B/CR/M
Diarrhoea	Cypress	C/M
Earache	Camomile.Lavender.	C
Eczema	Camomile.Juniper.	B/CR/M
Fainting	Peppermint.	I
Feet (aching)	Lavender.Lemongrass.Peppermint.	F/M
Flatulence	Coriander.Fennel.Peppermint.	M
Fluid Retention	Fennel.Juniper.Rosemary.	B/M
Frigidity	Jasmine.Neroli.Rose.Ylang-ylang.	B/M
Haemorrhoids	Cypress.Frankincense.Myrrh.	B/CR/M
Hair Loss	Bay.Cedarwood.Rosemary.	M
Hangover	Fennel.Juniper.Rosemary.	B/M
Hay Fever	Eucalyptus.Hyssop.	I/V
Headache	Lavender.Peppermint.	C/M/V
Heartburn	Anise Star.Peppermint.	M

64

Disorders	Essential Oils	Methods of Application
Heat Rash	Camomile.Lavender.	B/CR
Hot flushes	Geranium.Sage.	B/M
Hyperactivity	Camomile.Vetivert.	B/M/V
Immune system	Eucalyptus.Lavender.Tea Tree.	B/M
Indigestion	Anise Star.Fennel.Peppermint.	M
Inflamed glands	Camomile.Lavender.	C/I
Influenza	Eucalyptus.Niaouli.Pine.Thyme.	I/V
Insect bites and stings	Camomile.Lavender.	CR/N
Insect repellent	Clove Leaf.Peppermint.	V
Insomnia	Neroli.Lavender.	B/I/M
Irritability	Camomile.	B/M/V
Itchy skin	Camomile.Lavender.	B/CR/M
Laryngitis	Benzoin.Thyme.	I/M
Lice	Eucalyptus.Tea Tree.	M
Mastitis	Geranium.Rose.	C/CR/M
Menopause	Clary sage.Geranium.Sage.	B/M
Mental fatigue	Basil.Peppermint.Rosemary.	B/I/V
Migraine	Lavender.Peppermint.	C/M/V
Mouth ulcers	Myrrh.	N
Muscular aches	Ginger.Marjoram.Rosemary.	B/C/M
Muscular spasm	Camomile.Lavender.Rosemary.	B/C/M
Nailbed infection	Tea Tree.	N
Nappy rash	Camomile.Lavender.	CR/M
Nausea	Anise Star.Ginger.Peppermint.	I
Nettle rash	Camomile.Lavender.	CR/M
Neuralgia	Camomile.Marjoram.Rosemary.	CR/M
Nightmares	Frankincense.Neroli.	B/I/M

Disorders	Essential Oils	Methods of Application
Palpitations	Frankincense.Melissa.Ylang-ylang	B/M/V
Periods:		
Heavy	Cypress.Geranium.	C/M
Irregular	Clary Sage.Rose.Sage.	C/M
Painful	Clary Sage.Marjoram.Sage.	C/M
PMT	Camomile.Geranium.Rose.	B/M/V
Psoriasis	Camomile.Juniper.	B/CR/M
Rheumatism	Camomile.Coriander.Ginger.	B/C/M
Ringworm	Eucalyptus.Tea Tree.	B/CR/M
Scabies	Cinnamon.Coriander.	B/CR/M
Sciatica	Camomile.Lavender.	B/C/M
Shingles	Camomile.Eucalyptus.Tea Tree.	B/CR/M
Shock	Camphor.Neroli.Ylang-ylang.	I/V
Sinus	Eucalyptus.Hyssop.Pine.	I/V
Skin:		
Dehydrated	Geranium.Neroli.Sandalwood.	CR/M
Dry	Geranium.Rose.Sandalwood.	CR/M
Oily	Bergamot.Cypress.Mandarin.	CR/M
Mature	Carrot Seed.Frankincense.Neroli.	CR/M
Normal	Neroli.Rose.	CR/M
Sensitive	Camomile.Jasmine.Neroli.Rose.	CR/M
Sore throat	Benzoin.Niaouli.Sandalwood.	I/M
Spots	Lavender.	CR/I/N
Sprains	Lavender.Marjoram.Rosemary.	C
Stretch marks	Lavender.Neroli.	CR/M
Sun burn	Camomile.Lavender.Peppermint.	B/CR/M

66

Disorders	Essential Oils	Methods of Application
Thrush	Cinnamon Leaf.Myrrh.Tea Tree.	CR/M
Tonsillitis	Benzoin.Eucalpytus.Thyme.	I/M
Toothache	Clove Leaf.	N
Travel sickness	Anise Star.Ginger.Peppermint.	I
Varicose veins	Cypress.	C/CR
Verrucas	Lemon.Melissa.Tea Tree.	CR/N
Vertigo	Basil.Rosemary.	I/M
Warts	Lemon.Tea Tree.	CR/N
Whitlow	Tea Tree.	N

USAGE CODES:

B	-	BATH
C	-	COMPRESS
CR	-	CREAM
F	-	FOOTBATH
I	-	INHALATION (or facial steaming)
M	-	MASSAGE (full body or local application)
N	-	NEAT
V	-	VAPORIZATION

Essential oils can be used singly or as a blend of two or three, as indicated for each disorder.

NOTE TO THE READER

The contents of this booklet do not replace medical treatment. When in doubt or if symptoms persist, consult your general practitioner.

Essential oils are very concentrated and should be used with care.

Do not use undiluted essential oils on the skin (except where indicated).

Keep out of reach of children.

Keep away from eyes.

Some people may have an allergic reaction to some essential oils.

The following oils may cause photosensitivity and should not be used before sunbathing, as they may cause pigmentation of the skin:

Bergamot, Lemon, Lime, Mandarin, Orange

The following list indicates essential oils that may irritate the skin when used in massage or baths and should be used in a lower concentration:

Aniseed, Basil, Camphor, Cinnamon, Clove, Hyssop, Lemon, Lemongrass, Lime, Melissa, Nutmeg, Orange, Peppermint, Sage and Tea Tree.

Pregnancy - Extra caution should be taken during pregnancy, especially during the first few months. Seek professional advice regarding the use of essential oils.

FURTHER INFORMATION

Essential oils can be obtained from health food shops and some chemists.

For your nearest supplier, or if you have trouble obtaining essential oils, telephone **Natural by Nature Oils** on **020-8202 5718.**

Natural by Nature Oils Ltd.
The Aromatherapy Centre
9 Vivian Avenue
Hendon Central
London   NW4 3UT
England

Oils and Advice: **020-8202 5718**
Clinic: **020-8201 5555**

'There is a remedy for every illness to be found in nature.'
Hippocrates (460-377BC)